How to make

Your
Home
Your
Sanctuary

by K.L. Lyons

Chapbook Press

Schuler Books
2660 28th Street SE
Grand Rapids, MI 49512
(616) 942-7330
www.schulerbooks.com

How to Make... Your Home Your Sanctuary

ISBN 13: 9781966196068

Library of Congress Control Number: 2024926935

Printed in the United States by Chapbook Press.

Before words...Dedications

I dedicate this book to all homemakers: wife, husband, mother, father, single person, grandmother, or grandfather.

I also dedicate this book to honor the Holy Spirit of God in thanksgiving for His insight given to me.

A Sanctuary Defined:

A sanctuary is a building, a room, or a space that provides safety and protection.

—Merriam-Webster

Another thought regarding a sanctuary...

"You are my refuge, a fortress where my enemies cannot reach me"

Psalm 61:13 NLT

And yet another...

"Therefore, whosoever heareth these sayings of mine, and doeth them: I will liken him unto a wise man,who built his house upon a rock."

Matthew 7:24 KJV

Contents

The Artist, The Creator

You are the artist, the creator.

As Erwin Raphael McManus explains in his book, *The Artisan Soul:* "We all carry within us the essence of an artist. We need to create, to join in bringing something beautiful, good and true; in order for our souls to come alive."

Thinking of McManus' words, I came to realize that the true Artist is our Creator. Before I was born the Creator knew me. He knew my talents, my shortcomings, my general humor, my health. He knew all about me. He created me.

GOD is the master Artisan of our lives. We individually bring care to the process of making and creating. This process is very evident in our home as we create the place in which we want to live every day. This is the place we want to wake up in each morning; and the place we want to rest in at the end of the day. We each have the God-given ability to make our home a work of art.

Whether we construct on an automotive assembly line, or teach in a classroom, it is true. Whether we are stylists at a salon, an IT specialist, or a house builder; it is true. Whether we bake bread, preach God's word or write books; it is true. As the human spirit moves toward spiritual health; he realizes that this is true. The artisan process of creating is better for the soul than any other activity in which we could ever be involved. We are not just a hive of busy bees mindlessly doing, doing, doing. God chooses us; as He creates us in His image. We are born to create. It is in this process that we come to life; we keep growing. And on this journey, we realize that because we are born to create, we can—for sure—create the home that we have dreamed of in our minds.

In this book you will find principles of interior design and many suggestions to accomplish this. So, let's get started!

Your Front Door

We will start with the street view of your home; as we walk up to the front door and surrounding space.

Does it look welcoming? Is it neat, clean and inviting? Does it beckon you in? A seasonal wreath on your door or perhaps a potted plant next to your door can tell all that you are happy here. The recently popular wooden stand-up welcome signs are another option; as is a chair, a pair of chairs, or a bench.

It's great to combine some of these items into an attractive venue. Making this first-impression space attractive says that you care. It is a way of saying "Knock or ring and come in!" It need not be expensive or costly. It need not be a large space. It just needs to tell you that someone welcoming lives here and is glad to see you. Think about what will work in the space you have; about what you would like to do with the space. It's not unusual to try more than one arrangement to get it right.

The color of your front door does not always have to match your interior colors. Sometimes if you live in a condo or an apartment; you have no choice about the color of your door. Natural wood stain-colored doors never lose their charm. Yellow is a happy color. Is the choice yours? If so, just pick a favorite shade that you would love to see each time you open the door or drive up to your home. If there is a window or windows in your front door; make sure they are always clean and shiny.

A popular option now is to have a punch code to unlock your front door. This is highly efficient for you not to have to fish in your pocket or purse for keys. It is also easier for children and teens to not to have to be concerned about a key to the front door. You teach them the 3 or 4 digit code to punch in and they're always able to get inside if there is no parent or person in charge to open the door. When you go out for a walk you just leave your door locked with no concern about getting back in. This punch code mechanism is often found near the garage door or right on the front door. It can be programmed to open the garage door. You control who knows the code and you can change it if you wish.

As an interior designer, however, I must admit that my personal preference is that a keypad is not as interesting as a beautiful shade found in nature. You can however add a lovely brass knob and a brass kick plate at the bottom of your front door to take it up a notch.

So let's get started with what to do after you enter your home. Think about what the word "home" means to you. What it meant to you as a child. What made it "home"? What does this word mean to you now? What would you like it to mean?

Principle: The goal is to make your front door and any area around it look attractive and welcoming.

What is Home?

Home is:

- A blessing
- A place set apart from the troubles of the world
- A gift to you, for you and yours
- A place to gather
- A place to rest
- A place to heal
- A place to cook and bake and enjoy food
- A place to share
- A place of joy
- (and especially) A place to pray

Home is many things to you and to each person who may be living with you. It means so many different things to each one of us.

Mostly home is a place to rest, and to recoup from the work of the day. It is a place that when you come in and close the door behind yourself. You can take a deep breath, exhale, and say "I'm home!" You kick off your shoes, check the mail, and think about the relaxing evening stretching out before you. Leave any unresolved issues of the day on the other side of the door; while you think about the achievements of the day; as well as the plans for tomorrow. You don't leave the good thoughts on the other side of the door. You welcome them in with you.

Principle: Home should and can be a welcoming place, wrapping its arms around you like a big hug!

There are definite strategies to make your home your welcoming place, your sanctuary, a place of peace, your place of joy. The purpose of this book, and what you will learn in reading it, is just how to make your home exactly this.

You can create the home you want. Rome wasn't built in a day. While you are not building Rome—nor do you have an army helping you—think of decorating your home as a process. Often, like growing, it is a never-ending process. But the fun is in the planning process, and in the doing, working toward the elusive finished product.

It really doesn't matter if your home is a one-room efficiency or a 20-plus-room mansion. The size is not important.

Principle: It's really all about the emotion you feel at what you feel upon entering, that causes you to sigh that deep contented feeling.

It also doesn't matter whether you are the only person living there, or if there is a brood living with you. Often the more people there are, the more fun and merriment there is. And of course, the more challenges. It is your choice! Our daily environment influences our energy level, attitude, peace of mind (or lack thereof), and many other facets of our personality. Your home is ever evolving to meet your and others' needs. In other words, "Is it you? Does it speak to you what you want to hear?"

Principle: As these needs change; so, does the interior of our homes.

Simple or ornate, and all in between is truly an individual choice. It has to do with many principles of interior design. Mostly it has to do with what we, as individuals, love to see and feel when we walk into this space of ours. How does this space make us feel?

The purpose of this book is to introduce and develop with you, what you want in your space—as well as how to achieve the specialness of making YOUR house uniquely YOUR home.

Assessing Your Home

Simply put, every house has four walls, a door and windows minimally. A grandiose house may have numerous entrances and a wall of windows overlooking a breath-taking view. It may also have many rooms on various levels. Your home may be a little more humble. It may simply be a three-room efficiency. Whatever the size, it is yours and there are so many choices to make as you put your special touch to your home. It takes time and thought and perseverance to make a house your home. It reflects you, your values and your treasures as you fill it with the things you love. Your home provides the background for the life you are living.

Interior design is a work in progress. Decor is unique to each of us. For instance, in choosing color, one may see aqua, another sea-foam green, and yet another true green. While these can be thought of as different names for the same basic color, there are distinct differences in the various hues of the same color. However we see it, color has a huge influence on how we think and feel. What we see first when we walk into a room is the "big" picture. This includes but is not limited to: light, color, arrangement, and function. Walls and windows are quickly noticed. There are many, many architectural variances in homes.

Some of us have been creating our "nest" for many decades. Others are just beginning. We learn as we go. There is one cardinal rule to keep in mind as we go forward: ***form follows function.*** Defining the function of each space will make many future decisions much easier. Sometimes this is obvious as in the kitchen and the bathroom. Sometimes it is not so obvious as in the newer models of homes without many walls; or when we re-purpose a bedroom as an office, or a playroom, or a media room. Just remember: you have the ability to make it all work the way you want. Whatever stage you are in life—and whatever stage your home is in—ask yourself these questions, as you enter your home:

Is there a permeating attitude you feel, one of gratitude and love?

Is a general feeling of happiness or contentment evident?

Do you feel safe and secure here?

Is this a place in which you will be able to grow: physically, health-wise, a place of nourishment for body, soul and spirit?

Is it a place to get a good night's rest?

Is it a place of comfort?

Is it a place to enjoy a simple meal or a more lavish dinner as your mood or a holiday suggests?

Does it provide space for your hobbies and room for the tools of your trade—your favorite interests?

Does it provide a place in which to create?

Answering these questions with a "Yes" is not a given, but must be intentionally thought about and figured out. This you can do with some simple interior design principles—plus, thought, effort, and patience. These principles and guidelines will follow in various chapters of this book. There are some tried-and-true rules in home design, but consider them just suggestions. Use only what makes sense to you!

What appeals to you? Or if you are brave and willing to take a risk, climb out of your box and try something new and different. Whatever you do, have fun!

Always remembering that you were born, in His image, to create—this is an indisputable truth. And do have fun in this process. Think about the colors you like, the ones you go to time and time again. This will provide you with your color palette. Choosing your color palette can be difficult with so many choices of colors, shades, and hues available to you. There are some ways to make this choice easier. These you will find next.

Your Color Palette

Decisions! Decisions! Decisions!

Deciding on your color palette is one of the most difficult decisions to make. There are so very many shades and hues available to you. We just cannot use them all! There are six basic colors: red, orange, yellow, green, blue, and purple. Black is actually a total of all six basic colors. White is the absence of all color. From these six colors, hundreds of various hues can be mixed; with resulting shades you will like or even love. Many you will not be attracted to whatsoever—you just plain won't like them at all. And that's ok, it's good to recognize that fact.

There are several options that you can use to help decide on your color palette. These are listed below.

First, paint stores have many, many strips of assorted colors. Each of these strips can be found with complimentary shades right next to them. These thin cardboard strips are free. Pick up those that appeal to you the most; but no more than six. More than six will just lead to confusion and frustration.

Another way is to notice colors and shades when you visit friends' homes. Really look around and make mental notes of shades you are attracted to. Notice which shades are used as accents, used in much smaller amounts. These are the colors you see on throw pillows, vases, flowers, picture frames and other decor items.

There are also obvious textures in the room: the feel of the upholstery, the floor covering, hard or soft? Always be conscious of which hues are plentiful and which are used sparsely.

Thirdly, another quick and simple way to note your preference is to simply open your closet door. Stand back—what colors do you see the most? These are a big clue for you because these are the shades you have chosen time and time again as you have purchased clothing.

A fourth way is to peruse home interior design magazines. You will find pictures of completed rooms with dominating as well as accent colors. One strong suggestion—other than black and white—three colors in one room are sufficient. Use different shades of the three colors you choose. This fact can be true of the other rooms in your house as well. You change the order around as to which shade dominates and which shades support the dominating one.

Fifth, online finished rooms are available for you to view. These programs are lots of fun to watch and highly informative as well.

Lastly, HGTV and magazines present to you online hundreds of ideas. Bigger ideas like knocking down walls or relocating them always must be assessed by a builder. It's necessary to work with a professional, licensed, insured builder to tackle this kind of project. There are various building codes, rules and inspections. Window treatments and furniture arranging can be accomplished by you. All it takes is to become familiar with basic interior design principles and perseverance! Home decorating magazines and books can be found at the library or your local bookstores.

It is of value to consider the colors used in commercial buildings, such as coffee shops and restaurants. These shades have been chosen by color experts. Such experts verify the psychology of how colors affect people. Different colors definitely have an effect on each of us. We are drawn to certain colors, which then become our favorites.

All About Paint

Painting Walls and Trim

It is extremely important to realize that colors in large commercial settings, under fluorescent lights will not look the same on your walls or even on your furniture. Colors used in clothing, upscale stores and boutiques and restaurants do influence you. We use this fact to help us determine our color palette. We want to determine the color we see the most of when walking into a room. This is most likely the walls and other large areas such as the floor and bigger furniture pieces. We hardly ever notice the ceiling color unless it screams at us to be noticed. It is generally white, or off white, or a very light shade, almost white of any color.

An important step in determining our wall colors is to buy a sample size of the colors you like the most. Paint a substantial, at least 3x4 feet square on different walls in the room or area you are decorating. It is imperative that this step be followed. The results will most likely be miles apart from how the shade looks in the store and how you expected it to look.

The lighting in your home changes the hues with natural light, or other lighting options being used in the evening hours. There is a critically important step. You do not want to go to the expense or the effort of having an entire room re-painted again because you did not test it with a color sample paint first.

With these techniques, you will soon find a palette of 3-4 shades of colors that will work for you. One of these shades will be used often, as the color on most walls and perhaps large, upholstered furniture pieces, It is a helpful idea to carry these colors on a paint card strip(s) with you as you shop for other things you will be buying to complete your room or area.

Darker Colors and Lighter Walls

Darker walls, such as navy or emerald green have a different effect on us than lighter tones. Darker walls feel intimate, rich, and secure. Dark colored walls have a definite impact on your mood. They make you feel safe, protected, and at rest. They also tend to close you in. Lighter walls are airier and fresher. If you're terribly confused, even after you've painted your large sample, you can go with contrasting walls. One or two of the walls may be dark and the others lighter. This takes a little more daring than the safe way of all-matching walls. However, it can certainly provide much more interest and drama. It is also a little easier to find other decor pieces, ready-made upholstered furniture, or window treatments to work together well. This is because you have a much wider color range from which to choose.

Principle: Go with the lighter shade because this is easier to work with as you make additional required decisions.

Again, You do not want to go to the work or expense of re-painting walls every couple of years.

This is truly a matter of individual choice as one person may want things to look flamboyant, extremely interesting while a different person prefers a much calmer environment. I was raised in the same size three-bedroom colonial as my husband. I have five siblings. He has one. I prefer calm, open colors. He prefers darker shades. I've often wondered if the number of people in the same size home has influenced this. Who knows? We each have a private space where we feel that we can be alone to decompress and pray.

Trim Work & Wall Color

The trim work around the door and windows, as well as around the floor and ceiling, may either match or contrast with the wall color—depending on your preference.

Principle: In rooms that flow together, use the same color or shade of trim work throughout.

Actually, it's often good to use the same color of trim work throughout your home, in various rooms. This provides a unifying effect, minimizing confusion. There is a product available for the upper molding trim around the top of the wall just touching the ceiling, that is much lighter in weight and easier to install than the typical wood product. It is available at big box stores..

If the budget is a concern, it is not unusual to have no molding to separate the wall from the ceiling. You can always add it later. Adding ornate woodwork up high definitely has a richer effect, whether the room is small or large. I have even seen painting used to mimic wood trim up high. It was really real-looking and almost made me want to reach up and touch it to believe it was done with paint, not real wood.

How Much Paint Is Needed?

So now after deciding on your palette, your wall and woodwork color, you are ready to paint! Get your brushes and roller pan out or call the professional painter. Estimate how much paint you will need by walking off how many feet you are going to cover. No need to measure accurately down to the inch. Using your own foot as a guide, pace off the length and width of the room. Multiply the length times the width to give you the approximate SF (square feet) of the room.

For example, If the room is 10 feet wide by 14 feet long; multiply 10 X 14 = 140 feet. A gallon of paint covers 200 SF of wall space. This will vary if you are covering a dark red wall with a soft beige shade. So for a 10 x14 SF room; you will use just under a gallon. You can figure on two, or sometimes even three coats of paint if you are covering a dark color with a noticeably light one. Take your room size into the paint store as well as your color cards with your final choices. If your room is not square, rectangle, or has interesting alcoves, the painters in that department are willing to help you figure out how much paint you will need for walls and woodwork.

Paint Finishes

Paints have various finishes and they vary on how they reflect the light. The finish may be flat, eggshell, or semi-gloss to gloss. These finishes each have different light refraction and different washability to clean finger marks or other stains on the wall.

Eggshell is the preferred finish for living room, dining room, bedroom and hallway walls.

Semi gloss is used in the kitchen and bath, to make it easier to wipe away splashes, smoke and grease build up. These rooms also need a higher light refractability. In these rooms, we need all the light we can get as we get ready to put makeup on faces to go out and meet our public, one might say! We also need as much light as we can get as we read recipes in the kitchen and use the stove and microwave. Safety is extremely important. This finish is also used on door and window sashes.

Flat finish paint is generally only used on the ceiling because it is not touched, by fingers or anything else. It does not need to be repainted as often as walls. The ceiling paint will easily last 8 years before it needs to be repainted. The exception to this is the kitchen ceiling if smoke or grease stains are visible.

Isn't it exciting that you are finally ready to start? The actual painting process of getting the paint on the wall goes much quicker than trying to choose colors, shades, and hues. Congratulations! Usually, two coats are needed to give a good coverage. But again, as stated earlier this does depend on the difference between the new and former colors.

The woodwork may take a little longer depending on the size because it usually must be brushed by hand instead of rolling the paint on the wall. Colors used impacts all of this. White premade woodwork and trim are available at big box home stores.

You are ready now to move the furniture out of the room or into the middle of the room. Cover it to avoid any splashes or drips. This step seems very basic. But knowing human nature, most of us just want to get on with the job. We want to get finished so that we can put our room back together.

Patience is truly a needed virtue in painting our walls. You do not want to ruin your sofa, chair, or table or lamp by rushing. There are inexpensive lightweight plastic covers to put over your furniture available at the paint or dollar stores.

Professional drop cloths are very protective; but they are also more costly and very heavy to use. So, consider these facts before you go to the expense of buying them,

As you finish the painting, always keep a small amount of wall paint and woodwork paint in an airtight container to use for touch ups when needed. Now onto the much more finishing details, giving your room a cohesive look. Next for one of the more fun parts: the furniture.

Furniture

The kitchen and dining area run a close second in use to the great room. Often in newer floor plans, these three functions: visiting, cooking, and eating run together. Wall colors, floor coverings and moldings are repeated throughout to provide consistency and minimize distraction.

Some of these comments may seem self-evident but recalling them is always good. Furniture also generally has a specific function assigned to it. The sofa and upholstered chairs are made for sitting, to relax alone, or for visiting with others.

The table and chairs in the dining area are made for serving and sitting down. Dining chairs without arms use space well because they can be pushed under the table when eating is finished.

Principle: Take your time in purchasing. Do buy only what you love, but make sure it fits you.

Comfort is paramount. Color and pattern are second. Light tones and neutrals are much safer in choosing larger expensive upholstered pieces. Different shades can then be introduced, used, and changed at a much lower cost than buying new furniture. These additional colors are brought into the room with such items as throws, pillows, and decor items.

Seating for Comfortable Dining

Dining chairs that are all wood, with no upholstered parts, are common. But are they comfortable? If your lifestyle includes sitting around the table and chatting after a meal, think this over. While these chairs are much easier to keep clean than upholstered dining chairs, it's just not worth it if you and your family and friends are uncomfortable. The back may not feel good to you and often, the wood has no give. There are chairs available with different structured backs not always visible to the naked eye, which can be comfortable. This is why it is so important to try the chair out. We often tend to sit at the table after eating. Backless benches in beautiful woods to match the table are popular and interesting. They do serve a growing family well. But they are also the last place adults want to sit. You can always relegate the bench to serve as a coffee table or a hall bench as your children approach adulthood. Then purchase a softer host and hostess chair for either end of a rectangular table, or to use right across from each other if using a round or oval dining room table. You for sure don't want to end up with anyone having a backache because they were not comfortable for an hour or so sitting, eating and talking.

Great Room Furniture

There are guidelines to purchasing upholstered, comfy furniture for these rooms. Sofas generally come in three standard sized lengths: six feet, seven feet, or eight feet. If you would like a longer sofa, it will need to be custom-made. Always, always measure your space before you buy. Bring out the masking tape to measure the space your sofa or sectional will take up. Put the tape on the floor where you intend to place your sofa. Be sure that there is enough space to walk around a coffee table to reach your sofa without bumping something.

When arranging occasional seating chairs, it's important to have a spot to put a cup of coffee, a drink or a book within arm's reach of where folks will sit.

One of the more challenging rooms to decorate is the living or great room. These rooms vary in size, location in the home, and in function. Watching TV, reading, writing, doing homework, puzzles, visiting with guests, snacking and even snoozing occurs. Windows may be prevalent with boundless natural light or not too plentiful.

Sometimes a fireplace is in the room as well. Because this is the room that family members use the most for so many varied functions; take your time to visualize what furniture you would like; and where you would place it.

The living room or great room of your home should seat at least six people. Sofas may have loose-back pillows or sewn-in pillows. Loose-back pillows give you more flexibility by turning the back pillows to wear more evenly. These may also be removed if you are using the sofa as a bed for an overnight guest. Removing the back pillows gives you the width of a twin bed for your guest.

Many great rooms have a fireplace to consider. As you plan, do not always automatically think that the fireplace belongs in the living room space. It can be very cozy in the dining room or give special warmth to a sunroom on cold dark evenings.

There are in-wall fireplaces that don't take up floor space in the room. Electric fireplaces have also become very popular. They can be moved to wherever there is an electrical outlet. Most can generate extra heat as well. It's always fun to decorate the mantle. Consider the height of the mantel as there are many variances. If you have a wall model, a mantle can be added above it, right on the wall. It should be at least one foot above and extend a foot or two beyond the actual fire image.

Decorating the mantle can be done in symmetrically or asymmetrically. Symmetry calls for the same or very similar decor items placed close to either end of the mantle. It is your choice. Symmetry speaks of organization. Asymmetry is seen to be more interesting. In an asymmetrical arrangement, there would be different items of different sizes at either end of the mantle.

Candles, books, photos, and special keepsakes look interesting on the mantle and tell a little story about you. Behind these items a mirror also can add interest. Multiple mirrors of varying shapes work well also. They may be hung on the wall simply propped on the mantle. If propped, put a little sticky round in front of the mirror so that it won't slide off the mantle if a door happens to catch wind and slam shut. Or better yet, hang the mirror securely on the wall. When deciding what to place on the mantle, also consider: how much space there is from mantle to ceiling, and large objects, whether they be architectural pieces, paintings, candles or candelabras. Whatever you choose, fewer large pieces are much more interesting than many smaller items.

Great Room Seating

Wrap-around sectionals seat more people but do take up more room. Sometimes it is a bit awkward to get to the middle of a wraparound sectional once it is placed in your home. When viewing it in a spacious furniture store, it is easy to reach the middle section. Note the traffic pattern. Will people have trouble walking around? That is where the masking tape on your floor helps.

As you use masking tape to outline the dimensions of the furniture you would like, it helps you to figure out if all will fit comfortably in your room. Is there one entrance into the room or multiple? Traffic patterns should be kept clear to avoid "collisions".

TV Entertainment Centers

Unless you are blessed with a dedicated media space, your great room is also where the TV and various components are found. As you dream about your new sofa, after you've decided the length, consider the natural lighting of the area. Are windows and/or sliders directly opposite the TV? This may present a problem during the day with reflections making it very difficult to see the picture. Window treatments can usually solve this for you.

Entertainment center cabinets usually are constructed with storage space as well. This space may be open or closed with glass or solid doors. Shop around until you find what will work best for you. The faux fireplace may be included in the entertainment center.

Artwork, Pictures, and Photos

Most homes have a sofa and chairs in the great room, as well as the ever-present TV. It is the artwork in your space that defines your personality.

Buy pictures that speak to you, that you want to gaze at rather than just noticing. It does much to truly make your home YOUR home. It is distinctive to you. It does not have to fit into your color scheme. If you love it, use it. It will give you pleasure every time you look at it. But you absolutely must love it to hang or place it in your home.

Photos of the people you love, even photos of your pets put your stamp on the room. Artwork may be hung on the wall, placed on a sofa table or end tables or even placed on a decorative easel if you have a spot for it. The artwork—whether it be framed or unframed canvas, watercolor behind glass, or photos—must have meaning to you. Yourself, your family and your friends will enjoy it as well. It is special to you, so it will be special to all who see it. The photo may be large or small, or a grouping of smaller photos. It is not necessary that frames match, although matching frames give you a more completed look.

Or you may prefer a collection of photos hung on a blank wall. If you are using smaller pieces, lay them out on the floor before hanging. A straight pin will hold up to five pounds. I tend to move my art around as the spirit hits me. This gives me a new appreciation for what I have as I view it in a different spot.

Artwork need not be costly. It can be your young child's drawing or painting that means a lot to you. You can find interesting pictures not only at art museums, but also at garage sales and resale shops. One of my favorite pictures I have is a picture of a playground slide, covered with snow in the wintertime. It is done in whites, blues and grays. It tells me that summer is coming even though it's cold and snowy now.

Favorite un-posed photos of loved ones laughing and having fun are also very effective. I became tired of our wedding picture and put it away for a while. In its place I used a picture of my husband eating the last spoonful of his favorite ice cream flavor from a five-gallon tub that we bought from the dairy. It barely fit in our freezer. It makes me smile every time I look at it.

Decor Items

To make your dwelling place uniquely your own, display items, photos, pictures, paintings, or your favorite scriptures. Otherwise, even if it was a gift to you, don't display it unless you love it. It's so easy to end up with way too much clutter. When this happens, you can't enjoy what you're looking at. The result is total sensory overload. Seasons in the climate change, just as the seasons in your life change.

Fashion changes. Be ever ready to purge and change. Irreplaceable items should be protected especially when you pack them away even for a short period. You can change out your decor items as you please.

Don't be afraid to re-gift or donate those things that don't speak to you, that are not special to you. If you have too many, change them around. Pack some away, bring them out later. You don't have to display everything, all the time. We tend not to look at things that have been there for a long time—hardly seeing them anymore. To help this issue, you can just place certain things in a different place, thus, seeing them anew again! Too much, too many becomes clutter and subtracts from the peacefulness you are trying to achieve. Keep what you truly love—out goes the rest!

Considering Books

I am a lover of books. You may not be. I have books all over the place! Big coffee table books full of beautifully colored pictures, children's books, books of my favorite poems—on tables, on bookcases, even piled in a basket on the floor. I have been guilty of buying a book because I loved the color of the cover. This is not really recommended. But I still like it. If you're not in love with books to the extreme that I am, consider just having one or two interesting books as part of your decor. It could be a book that tells the history of your hometown, perhaps your Bible or a photo album. Any book that means something to you.

You can always open a recipe book to a yummy, colorful photo. Put that book in a small easel on your countertop, You can change the page of the book or even change the book according to seasons. I've heard it said that a room without a book is like a room without flowers: no soul!

Magazines help this cause as well. As you gather with others, your books often speak to others. They say more and can be heard more clearly than your own voice and words.

Remember that it takes time, effort and perseverance to find exactly the look that pleases you in every square foot of your room, and every corner. You will discover what look pleases you as you sit with your coffee or tea and look around at your domain; your castle—tiny, medium or lavish and large. Take the time so that when you've spent your day, you feel good when you open the door and walk in. This guideline bears repeating and repeating and repeating. It's your home—make it distinctively yours.

Window Treatments

As we progress through choosing our color palette, our furniture, our decor items and books, let's think about windows. The more of them the better!

Personally, I would love to have no window treatments at all. Unfortunately, this usually does not work, unless you live on huge acreage, for several reasons. Privacy is one major concern. Sun damage is another. This damage can be mitigated by pulling blinds when the sun is at its brightest, doing the most damage in fading your furniture or flooring.

Many different blinds are available, from the widely used style roller shades to duette fabric shades; or double or single cell blinds. Sheer fabrics on rods—or tacked right to the wall or woodwork— is especially cost effective, easy to install, and beautiful as sheers flutter in the breeze.

Heavy drapes, especially those with a lining to appear white from outside your home most likely require professional installation. Look through magazines and books to find the look you like and the ones you want to imitate. Cafe curtains that cover the lower half of the window provide interest without breaking the bank. They can usually be hung on tension rods inside the window frame. A matching or contrasting valance hung up high will complete the look. Go back and check your color palette.

Window treatments can blend into the wall tones or contrast with them. Be sure that when window coverings are being used, that they look attractive when closed or open. The rule for covering windows in fabric curtains or drapes is double to the expanse of the glass you're covering. If you scrimp on this guideline, it may look pretty tacky.

Inside Shutters

If shutters are being used as the window treatment, only the glass needs to be measured: height and width. Leave the exact measuring to the professionals. Shutters may be opened to let in more light, either in-place or hinged style. Shutters can be used in contemporary, traditional, country, and French country periods appropriately. They may be made of wood or vinyl. They may blend in or contrast with your wall and woodwork color. You can search them out in flea markets or have them custom made. Shutters add another dimension to your walls, making the room instantly more interesting. They also can provide more insulation on cold, freezing days. I have placed a six foot high shutter next to the door to the garage. The shutter is propped against the wall. I hung a lightweight mirror on the shutter. It is very practical in checking your appearance before leaving.

Whether it be a small 8x10 foot bedroom, office, reading room, prayer room, or whatever the space is dedicated to at this time, they add charm to the room. Shutters can be wiped clean with a damp cloth or dusted with a dry cloth. No washing like curtains in the spring, or having drapes cleaned. Once hung, they most likely will be permanent. You will absolutely love the versatility of shutters. So even though they can be costly at first, they are there to stay, usually never needing to be replaced as drapes, curtains, and shades do.

Take Stock: Time to Reassess

So how is your space coming? Are you getting there? Are you closer to the point where you can't wait to come home this evening, open the door and say "Aaahhhh I'm glad I'm home!"? Your home is welcoming you! Great job my friends! Now sit and walk around just noting what is really working for you and what perhaps needs a little tweaking. Be brave. Change things around if you get bored. Move a furniture piece to another room for a while if it can be re-purposed. Jot down your ideas on paper.

The Heart of the Home

The kitchen has often been referred to the as the "heart" of the home. It may well be that for you. It is a very important room because we eat to refuel our body. We give our body fuel so that you can take on the good—or maybe the challenges—of the day. In planning our home our kitchen deserves special attention. It may well be the most used part of the home—cleaning, organizing, cooking, baking, eating, preserving, school homework. Conversations with family and friends can occur in the kitchen. That is a great number of activities for one room to handle; therefore, every square inch should be used to support such activities.

Organizing is the priority in the kitchen. This is because the kitchen is such a busy place. Start with the storage options you have available. A place for everything and everything in its place.

Principle: the items you use most often, put within easy reach.

Dishes, mugs, and flatware can even be displayed on open shelves for a great, comforting look and quick access. Of course, not the service for twelve, but those that are used every day. Pots and pans, and specific electric items that you use every day or so, need to also be within easy reach. These can include, but not be limited to: coffee pot, air fryer, toaster, blender or whichever items you use most often. Group all your baking equipment together in one space. Try to put these items in a cupboard rather than on the counter. Some people with limited counter space even store baking pans in the oven. The more clear we can make the counter tops the easier it is on the eyes and on finding what we need. Sometimes we just need to ask ourselves how many different spatulas or skillets do we really use or need? Donate, give away, or toss whatever you don't need or use. I have a friend who gives away one thing each day so that she can keep the clutter down. I may have to start this practice because I love to wander through kitchen stores looking at all the gadgets available. I ask myself before I buy anything: "Do you really need this whatchamacallit?" Will I really use it, remembering that it has to be stored in a drawer or cupboard?

Countertops

Selecting your countertop is another exciting challenge in interior design. Counters are built into the kitchen, bath, and often in the office.

When choosing your countertops it is wise to choose a neutral color. This is true whether it be formica, slate, granite or cement. A neutral color for your countertop is advisable because it is not something that is changed every day. Your countertop is seen everyday, usually many times a day, because it is seen very quickly and continuously. Always, always, always also read and follow the directions to clean the countertops that are provided to you when you purchase them. If you don't have them, check google—a big help.

Dark colored counters look rich and sophisticated and show every little crumb. Lighter or multicolored counters are easier to keep clean. The best option if you're in a quandary is to go with either black or off white with few colored veins. Because it is such a costly item, don't be in a rush to make your choice.

To have a distinct color such as green or orange, you have limited options for other decisions. Color can easily be added to your countertops by what you place on them, be it fruit, sweets, flowers, or other decor items.

Whatever color you chose in your palette can easily be carried to your basic-colored countertops this way. Choosing a definite color other than black, beige, or white will not serve you well 5-6 years from now when you change your accent colors. It also does not enhance the salability of your home to have a dark blue or dark green countertop. That being said. I have a friend who has a dark green counter in a relatively small kitchen. She loves it—and it does look very nice. It is kept with few items on it to avoid confusion.

Storage in Your Kitchen

Do we ever have enough storage space in our kitchen? Or maybe it is better to ask the real question: what are we storing? Would it help us to go through and weed out those items we don't use at all, yet for some unknown reason we are holding on to? Time to let them go. If you haven't used it in a year, let it go, even the seasonal items. It's not so difficult to just say "goodbye" to it and let it move on to someone who was looking for something just like it.

Plates, bowls, glassware, flatware, pots and pans, bakeware, small appliances such as food storage containers, toaster, blender, mixer, pitchers, canned goods, mixes, and snacks all must have a home. Their home should not be ON the counter. You want to be able to clean your counter thoroughly after food preparation. This is impossible with a cluttered countertop. It also adds to mental confusion to see all of these items, or even many of them, or even one or two of them, if you have the cupboard space. Remember to donate or sell the items you don't use so that you can free cupboard space to get things off your counter.

You are especially blessed if you have a walk-in pantry. You can organize with things and food at your eye level. Items not used daily can be placed on higher shelves. Group like items together— all the baking items, snacks, even dishes and glassware, can be put on walk-in pantry shelves. Cookbooks are another item that can be arranged on the counter. Limit yourself to your favorite three cook books and put others away in a cupboard or bookcase. So many delicious recipes can be found online. However cookbooks do make interesting reading material. They usually have attractive pictures in them.

Principle: arrange your kitchen with items used the most to be readily accessible. Remember that you only have room for what you use.

Kitchen Linens

A place is needed for towels, placemats, table runners and perhaps tablecloths, which may be hung in a closet. Colorful towels, which work with your color palette, may be arranged in a basket to set on the countertop if room permits. This makes an attractive accent piece and makes the towels quickly accessible. A cookbook with a page open to a delicious picture of a main dish, salad or dessert can be placed on the countertop on a small easel. This can be changed seasonally as well.

Organizing your kitchen can seem to be a momentous task—it will be completed quickly using the principles above. It's worth the effort in completing an efficient organization because so many of your at-home hours are spent in the kitchen prepping, eating, and cleaning up. If it totally seems beyond you or if your time is extremely limited, you can do one of two options. Do it yourself a little at a time—it does not have to be completed all at once. Or you can also enlist a friend's help or pay someone to help you organize your kitchen shelves. Organizing is easy for some folks. Other people don't have a clue how to do so. Yet there's no question that items organized in your cupboard makes life much easier! Plus you will be using your space well and probably be surprised at how much more will fit in your cupboards.

The majority of accidents and injuries in the home occur in the kitchen. So it is important to note the safety of your kitchen. Practice simple habits such as: turning pan handles in toward the rear of the stove top to avoid catching them accidentally; checking to be sure burners and oven are turned off before food is served; keeping flammable items like hot pads and kitchen towels away from the stove top when cooking. Always use potholders, be they padded or vinyl ones, to pick up hot pans from stove top or oven. It's far better to develop this habit than to suffer a burn.

Bedroom and Bath

Use the same process and questions that we have used in our other spaces of your home. The one huge exception is that you must seek a comfortable bed. Give up other purchases for the time being to have a bed designed to give you a good night's sleep, Smaller purchases can always be added later. Use your color palette in the bedroom to create unity in your home. These may include nightstands on either side of bed, lamps (if overhead lighting is provided), artwork, and window treatments. Again remembering that safety is most important. Both of these rooms should have artwork or pictures in them.

Your bathroom especially needs things to soften the look because of all the gleaming hard built-in plumbing fixtures. Luxurious towels are worth the cost. Put a small succulent plant on the counter. Include a fluffy hand towel folded neatly on the vanity. Comfy rugs on the floor are not only attractive, but feel good on your feet if you get up at night. Again carry your color palette into your bathroom.

Your bedroom can and should be a place of refreshing calmness. This must be obvious to you when you enter your bedroom. Disarray makes it difficult to fall asleep. Take a few extra minutes to put shoes in the closet, to clear off your dresser or nightstand of items not needed at this moment. Make it all as simple and uncluttered as you can. This brings serenity and peace to your mind as you prepare to sleep.

Office Space

As work from home increases, so does the need for dedicated office area. Organizing is paramount in the office space. You may have a room as a home office, complete with lateral files and a gorgeous desk and comfortable desk chair. Or you may not. Clear plastic bins that hold hanging files can be found at most office stores. Organizational habits are as varied as eye colors. The goal is that you have a place to keep important documents such as diplomas, certificates, wedding licenses or any license for that matter should be placed in cardboard file folders. These folders can be inexpensive if purchased at dollar stores. Write the contents of the file on the top part normally used. Also write the contents on the top of the folder. You may be working with more than one folder at the same time. The exception of course is your driver's license. Put the directions and warranties for major purchases in a file folder(s) which can be found quickly. This is where important mail is kept: tax records, birth records and such. Utility bills, even if paid online automatically, should be kept. Some exceptions may be the garage door opener, which can be tucked into one of the horizontal supports of the door. The other exception may be the directions for the furnace which can be put in a Ziploc bag near the furnace. There are receipts for appliances and furniture that you would like to keep. The goal is to have someplace where your important documents are. You want to be able to find them. Keep it all in one place—even a dresser drawer if your space is tight.

Theater Room

How nice it is if you have theater room to view special movies and such. Nondescript walls will not distract viewers from the movie. Keep the furniture comfy and easy to clean. Leather or a man-made, stain-resistant fabric will serve you well. Lighting should be on a dimmer switch. You may want to have a compact fridge to keep drinks cold. A cupboard for non-perishable snacks would also be handy. Enough electrical outlets are a must. A bin for recyclables is good to have. A corn popper would be fun!

Think about what else you may like beside a huge 70- or 80-inch screen on the wall. Include a couple of warm throws, especially for wintertime watching. A few different size pillows should be available as well.

Flooring in this area should be easy to clean and maintain. No throw rugs are allowed because of the dim lighting, They could definitely be an accident waiting to happen. Relax and enjoy your special theater area.

Garage

The garage must be kept clean for critter control. Rubbermaid cupboards are available for purchase at most big box or hardware stores. They are easy to keep clean by wiping with a damp cloth or even hosing them down on a sunny warm day. Some have doors and some have drawers. Different sizes are available. Smaller tools can be stored in them. Larger outside garden tools, such as rakes and shovels, may be hung on wall brackets available at hardware stores. Even two-wheeled bikes may be hung up out of season.

Label drawers, bins or whatever you use for storage with a very visible label. Use thick black markers if possible. This will make it easier to find things like light bulbs, extension cords, etc. when you need them. If you don't want to use permanent markers on drawers, you can cut a blank piece of paper in half, write on it, and tape it to the bin or drawer. Doing so will keep your frustration level low. You won't have to hunt high and low for whatever you want.

Flooring is another consideration. There is a polymer composite available to be sprayed on the floor. It makes it much easier to keep clean than cement. It is an involved three-step process. Thus it is best to leave the installation to the professionals. While it looks attractive and is much easier to keep clean than cement, there is a caution. It can be slippery if wet from hose or wintry snow brought in on shoes and boots. Another flooring option is a one- or two-inch-thick rubberized product that comes in interlocking pieces. You could have fun and do a checkerboard pattern. These are comfortable and safe to walk on. They may be swept or cleaned with a hose.

Rear Outdoor Space

In this area we again go back to the basic questions of size and function. Go back and follow the process you used for interior rooms. Read the section that tells of the same process as you have used in building the other rooms in your home. Decide on the function: what will this space be used for? Outdoor space can become another area in which to live. How big is the area? Do you just want to read a book in solitude, while listening to the birds sing? Think about what will be happening in the space. Is it going to be a play area for young children? Or will you be eating out on a deck? There are flexible "ceilings" for your deck which you can adjust to control the sunlight. They can be found at Costco. Perhaps you'd like to plant a garden as your goal. Depending on the size of the yard that you have, you can set up spaces for various functions. If you want privacy, or if you want to hide something unattractive, such as trash cans or kids' toys; six-foot tall panels may be used. These may be cemented into the ground for year-round stability if desired. Or they may simply be placed in a hole 12-16 inches deep. The determining factors include the climate in which you live, and the location you want to put them in within your yard. There are fencing companies available to you to hire the job out for more permanence and stability. The gas company comes out to your home to stake out where gas lines are located. Call them before you start digging. There is no charge for this.

If you live in an apartment or condo, you may have a small deck, and no or little backyard. To provide privacy, buy 2 or 3 fake bushes or smallish trees. Place them to give yourself privacy depending on where your chairs, table, or lounge chair is. If you use real plantings, water often—every day or more than once per day in hot dry weather.

Whatever your choice is, do the research. But always, always have fun! Tackle one project at a time so as not to overwhelm yourself or your budget.

My wish for you is that you enjoy the process of making your home a peaceful place to be.

I trust that your home is now your sanctuary, that you absolutely love, love, love the finished look and feeling you have achieved—so that your home will always welcome you home!

Notes

On this page and the following pages, jot down your ideas about what you like and don't like. Think hard about it—use these pages as you develop your own distinct decorating plan and style.